The
PSYCHOLOGY
Of
SELLING

LESSONS ON WEALTH BUILDING AND PROVEN WAYS TO SELL ANY PRODUCT

JENNA AUSTIN

JENNA AUSTIN

TABLE OF CONTENT

INTRODUCTION

When my friends ask me how do I learn about business, the act of selling and wealth building, I usually say it's the zeal to become successful but it doesn't convince them at all, I guess looking back where I came from and my background is enough to ask the question over and over again.

Growing up in the 90s in a small town in Texas. People living around me and my family are just normal people with little pay around $100 or thereabout. On TV I will usually see rich people speaking, organizing seminars and talking about how they were able to achieve so much. I'll always think 'how did they do it'? But who will answer me then?

I had this zeal in me but I don't know what is it then, I could not understand it. I had to look for the successful people in my town and learn from them what they know. The first thing I was taught was how to have a positive and growing mindset. That alone changed how I saw things. I read books, listened to the little successful people in my town. One of them that own a store employed me and taught me how to approach customers, speak to customers to make them buy from you and also buy related items. I was also taught copywriting, how to write copy for advertisement for new products or goods that is not selling fine with discount offers. And that's how I found a new purpose in life.

I'm JENNA AUSTIN, a business coach, certified copywriter and sales expert. I've been in this industry for over 10 years. Trained a lot of individuals who have become gurus on their own.

The sole purpose of this book 'THE PSYCHOLOGY OF SELLING' is to teach you how you can grow your brand online, sell other people's product (Affiliate marketing), how to write copy for clients and make money and more importantly, grow your mindset.

JENNA AUSTIN

SECTION 1

EQUIP YOUR MINDSET FOR SUCCESS

You'll agree with me that growing in a small and remote town, my mindset wasn't really equip for success because of my environment and society and other factors I later discovered overtime. But how did I prevail over all that?

What you think of yourself is what you'll become. There's power in your thought, in your subconscious mind. Mindset is what separates the rich from the poor. When your mindset changes, your action changes, people will notice changes in you. It cannot hide.

It might sound easy as you're reading it but don't be fooled by its simplicity. It's not a one night kind success of thing, you need to actually put in the work. The good news is that you already have what it takes, which is YOURSELF.

Speaking about **MINDSET**, what is truly **MINDSET?**

MINDSET is a bunch of conviction frameworks that administers the way we think and act supported by the reality we have been exposed to.

Some factors that helped me have that mindset I needed for success.

THE ENVIRONMENT YOU FIND YOURSELF IN

Though I grew up in remote town, with a lot of "I know it all" mentality, bullies and like of them, I had to look for people who had this little understand as me. I don't really know much but from what I've watch and observe, there are different kind of people and I want to know those are successful than the rest of us in the same town.

So I set out and make acquaintance with the likes of them and my understanding changed overtime more than when I was spending time with the less successful people.

Envision yourself moving with 4 dummies, you'll eventually become the 5th dummy and not just that, you'll be the dumbest among them all.

Now imagine yourself moving around with 4 millionaires, you'll eventually become a millionaire and not just that, you'll likely become bigger than them.

It's time to review your actual space since it will straightforwardly impact your mindset and your mindset will set off your actions.

I was following people who had not much understanding as me and I was becoming worse than before but with little time I spent with those who had a well-equipped mindset, I found changes in me.

So if you were to inquire as to whether this has worked for me, I wouldn't falter to give you 1,000,000 occurrences both scholastically and business wise.

THE PEOPLE YOU TALK TO

People you spend time with, have fun together, discuss different stuffs together, all this have effect on your mindset either positive or negative.

During my teenage life in my town, I had a friend who hated online stuffs, I on the other hand don't really have much idea about online then. Then online has been this exposed as it is now, (thanks to technology) overtime, I started to hate online stuff too. I was ignoramus.

Envision yourself having companions who love discussing success, do you realize what will befall you? You will contact that sensation of success as well. Proudly vet your association and oust some personalities when vital.

When I started mingling with intellectual people, I became one of them.

BELIEVING IN YOURSELF

Believing in yourself is one of the most important step to having that successful mindset you need.

Before I made my 1st $100,000, I never believed I could do it at all. There was no atom of believe in me that I could get to such height. But what did I do to achieve that.

I had to be telling myself day and night that I can make it, I had to seeing the money in my account or savings, I had to write it down as a daily reminder to myself. I had to write down the strategies to use to make that amount I need.

I may not have made the $100k at my 1st trial but it changed my life and I saw myself hitting it on my 2nd trial and I did.

Our brain is wired in a way that anything you feed it with is what it gives you subconscious mind and your mind then finds a way to bring solution to that thing that you keep pondering about. That's why it's advisable to feed yourself with positive thoughts at all time.

LEARNING

People tend to shy away from learning new things because it's out of their comfort zone. Your comfort zone is like being stuck with all you know and be expecting a different results.

Continuous learning automatically grow your mindset, change is possible if we believe in it. Just because you're struggling right now doesn't mean you're not learning. Let me point out some things here:

DON'T BE AFRAID TO FAIL

To so many people, failure is like the end of the world. Relating to my story of how I couldn't meet goal of $100k. I failed to hit it but I learnt from my failure and tried again. Accepting failure will stop you from achieving great things.

MASTER NEW SKILLS

Mastering new skills can be very challenging but you need to understand that it doesn't just happen with the twinkle of an eye. Whenever you embark on learning a new skill, don't pressurize yourself over it. Give yourself time and you'll become good at it.

BE CURIOUS

Curiosity opens the mind to possibility you won't imagine on your own. When you ask "how did you do it?" your mind is trying to learn a new thing and not be stuck to one thing, indirectly growing your mindset

SECTION 2

21ST CENTURY ONLINE BUSINESS

When we talk about internet based business, what do we truly mean?

In this section, I'll be enlightening you regarding some web-based business you can do and make monstrous pay.

Business can just be characterized as, the demonstration of purchasing and selling of goods and services. Without intricacy, that's really the meaning of business.

What is online? Fundamentally, online is whatever has to do with the contribution of the web.

Online business has become the order of the day; a ton of youngsters across the world are presently exploiting the web in light of the fact that it's where the vast majority spend a most of their time.

Online business is the demonstration of carrying on with work online that implies the selling of goods and services on the web. The offline business and online business are practically comparable.

At the point when I began hankering for success monetarily, I chose to search on Google, I composed very much like the vast majority will do "How to make money online".

I saw a wide range of schemes and businesses, some looked genuine while some looked phony, after steady research, I've found a few solid web-based business anybody can do and begin making cash very quickly be committing time and energy to learning it, there are ;

1. Content marketing
2. Social media advertising
3. E-commerce
4. Online course teacher
5. Online mentor
6. Affiliate marketing

Allow me to clarify this couple of online business;

1. **CONTENT MARKETING**: This sort of marketing is a form of marketing focused on creating, publishing and distributing content (such as videos, blogs, social media

posts, eBooks etc.) for a targeted audience online.

This book is an illustration of content marketing in light of the fact that I'm giving you information as Text, this is an E-book.

I can similarly change over to sound or video and you will in any case get the same information.

2. **SOCIAL MEDIA MARKETING**: This kind of marketing deals with social media platforms and websites to promote a product or service.

Social media marketing is the internet based business of the 21st century that is flourishing and will keep on flourishing as long as individuals utilize the web. Marketing is the advertising of goods and services for likely clients to see and make a move.

3. **E-COMMERCE**: The term Electronic Commerce (ecommerce) refers to a business model that allows companies and individuals to buy and sell goods and services over the internet.

4. **ONLINE COURSE INSTRUCTOR**: In this age, information is vigorously wanted for and anybody that can bundle information and make it open will have enormous effect, build influence and furthermore get such a lot of money flow also relying upon the contribution. Online course is the bundling of information in

sound, video or text design for individuals who need that information.

5. **INTERNET COACHING**: In this age, Technology has made it conceivable to do numerous things on the web, one of them is individual to individual or individual's collaboration for all intents and purposes.

The internet coaching is truly flourishing and individuals on this train are truly making such a huge amount for themselves.

6. **AFFILIATE MARKETING**: Is an advertising model in which a company compensates third-party publishers to generate traffic or leads to the company's products or services. The third-party publishers are affiliates, and the

commission fee incentivizes them to find ways to promote the company.

This and a lot more are the internet business of the 21st century and some more. Our attention is on **MARKETING** and in the following sections we will disclose all you need to know about affiliate marketing.

SECTION 3

AFFILIATE MARKETING OF TODAY

So I went to the store to get a specific red and blue Nike air Jordan and I was simply moving between different lines like somebody that don't even know where he was going.

Individuals kept calling me to purchase from them since I was considered as a vagabond in the market.

A young fellow at last moved toward me and communicated to me, he inquired "what sort of Nike shoe are you searching for". Wow this fellow has been watching me stroll around and he was simply concentrating on my conduct very much like Facebook calculation.

He realized I was searching for a Nike, I felt vulnerable than to relate my concerns to him which was trouble in getting that specific color of Nike Air I was searching for.

I was so frightened of connecting with anybody since they will constantly climb their costs yet I needed to surrender.

Within a moment, he took me to a shop that had the very thing I was searching for, I got it right away, despite the fact that I spent over my financial plan, precisely the thing I was keeping away from yet stuffs occurs at some point.

As I left the shop, the person who brought me followed me and requested a tip, I gave him something and he said thank you, I don't figure he would invest energy carrying me to that shop and the owner wouldn't give him his commission.

Indeed, even in my own shop, I give commission for referring.

Are you actually searching for the meaning of **Affiliate Marketing**?

OK, Affiliate Marketing is just connecting a purchaser to the seller or vice visa, when the purchaser purchases; the connector gets a commission for so doing. Example is Amazon, amazon job is to connect me a book publisher to you the buyer, when you purchase a book amazon gets a commission.

In the affiliate marketing of today, your purpose is to assist others with selling their items involving the web as a vehicle to direct people to the offer.

Many individuals all over the planet are utilizing this plan of action to assemble their brands while making money. Personally, I've tasted affiliate marketing and the commissions have made me a few decent figures.

If you are that individual who is keen on making money on the web, and you don't have sufficient capital, then, at that point, you ought to as soon as possible consider affiliate marketing.

Observe somebody who has an item that is required and helpful to a specific crowd, settle with the owners or system, find out what being an affiliate for that organization involves, satisfy the measures and bet everything.

Why I like this business model is on the grounds that;

- Low cost of start-up; an affiliate does not require that you have an advertising team or purchase ad space to begin.

- It's a lucrative and far-reaching industry; affiliate marketing is a whole billion dollar industry. Such a wide field, it's pretty easy to look for a product.

- No expertise required in affiliate marketing; you don't need to be an affiliate marketing guru to succeed. Not immediately. This is a field where practice makes perfect.

- Its good as a supplementary source of income; with affiliate marketing, you don't need to quite from your job. At least not if you don't want to. You can use it as your side-line business

- You don't need to purchase the item before you can market.

- Independence. Flexibility. Convenience; affiliate marketing lets you work when you want to, if you want to. You're free to work in a flexible schedule and environment of your choosing.

Affiliate marketing is capital cordial and profoundly productive dissimilar to other business model.

SECTION 4

MAKING MONEY WITH AFFILIATE MARKETING

To make money from today's Affiliate marketing online is practically like making money with affiliate marketing offline. It is as yet unchanged instance of having an item you sell and searching for the clients who need them and after sale, you get your commission is basic and immediate as that, however, it will expect methodology to move toward the today's affiliate marketing.

This is what to think about prior to beginning your affiliate marketing business which are;

1. Picking a specialty: It's vital to pick a classification you like or energetic about. At the point when you like something you'll be adaptable in it.

2. Comprehend the affiliate program so well: Before you sign up for any affiliate program, address any outstanding concerns to find out about the technique for payment, currencies, long periods of payment, etc.

3. Always know your affiliate commission prior to marketing an item: Different item offers unique commission, be mindful so as to continuously figure out how much is appended to a specific item prior to marketing.

4. Affiliate link: When you join to an affiliate program, there is a particular link for any item you wish to market. Be mindful so as to copy your link accurately so that you wouldn't wind up marketing with someone's link. If you do that, you'll get no commission.

5. Originate your marketing procedure: Traffic is nearly all that you want to make a sale. Recognize where your potential clients are and run traffic that can empower you make sales or gather extraordinary leads.

6. Follow up: It takes a normal individual to see something at least a time or two to make a buy, so continue to follow up with email informing or direct informing.

For you to make money in affiliate marketing, these are the interesting points.

Examples of these affiliates platforms are; Clickbank. Amazon. Etc.

SECTION 5

ABILITIES REQUIRED FOR AFFILIATE MARKETING

Before you can get such a lot of money flow on affiliate marketing, you want to gain a few fundamental abilities that will help you in the course of your excursion as an Affiliate Marketer.

When I was beginning as an affiliate marketer, I knew for me to be effective, I expected to get familiar with some fundamental ability in the event that not I wouldn't encounter enormous achievement.

A portion of the abilities that helped me were;

Social Media Marketing (SMM): Social media marketing is the use of social media, the platforms of which people build social network to advertise your goods and services to get more sales, more customers and build a brand.

Copywriting: Copywriting is a way of writing text for the purpose of advertising or other forms of marketing. The purpose is to increase brand awareness overtime.

You can't actually sell online with zero information on copywriting. At the point when you realize this expertise and use it well, you'll convince individuals to purchase the item you are marketing.

Email Marketing: Email marketing is a form of marketing with that makes the customers on your email list to be aware of your product and service or even discount offers. Though it is an advanced level in affiliate marketing.

Leadership Abilities: Today's affiliate marketing requires your leadership for you to scale. You ought to be prepared to teach your crowd about what your program is presenting through essential means like transferred YouTube recordings, blog entry, online media post and coordinated internet based classes. Individuals that do this make more sales in affiliate marketing on the grounds that as they teach more individuals, they assemble their image for individuals to know and trust them.

Web Building: Another expertise that gives you an edge in today's affiliate marketing is your insight on web particularly funnel building. Some of the time you might be required to fabricate web pages to gather leads, rather than consistently paying a designer, it's shrewder to learn it assuming you are truly focused on the outcome of affiliate marketing.

SECTION 6

METHODOLOGIES TO SELL WITH AFFILIATE MARKETING

Selling the items you advertise on affiliate marketing can be testing particularly when you are a newbie in the industry, however I'm sure this section will assist you with addressing the issue.

Getting up one morning and posting your affiliate link for individuals to purchase what you are marketing isn't exactly an astute way of selling in the affiliate marketing business.

In this section; I'm going to show you shrewd methods of driving sales to your items and potentially selling.

Whatsapp Selling Technique: Whatsapp is a broadly utilized texting application that many individuals are utilizing to sell now. When you become the best at selling on whatsapp, you will experience gigantic sales, if you have the right crowd.

Four fundamental ways you can get sales through whatsapp are;

1. Whatsapp status
2. Direct message
3. Group message
4. Broadcast message

1. Whatsapp status: Many individuals will actually want to see your status as long as you have their numbers saved in your telephone and your number saved in their telephone.

So envision you have 5000 sorts of people's numbers saved your telephone, that implies over of 3000 will see your status while possibly not more and to make sales it's about driving traffic.

The more individuals that see your proposition, the probability of conversation that will occur.

2. Direct message: This is a compelling approach to likewise close a sale or sell your item. All you want to do is to send a composed message of what you are marketing. Don't make it voluminous, you can add emoticons and furthermore give spaces to make it simple for individuals to peruse

your proposal as far as possible and conceivably make a move.

3. Group message: This is the lodging of intrigued crowd in a whatsapp group that can contain a greatest measure of 256 individuals. When you communicate something specific more than one individual sees it, everybody in the group sees it. It can save you time rather than talking to every individual individually.

4. Broadcast message: This is the formation of list of a specific kind of crowd on whatsapp, for instance; you can make a list for everybody you just added to your contact list and send them a customized message to a limit of 256 individuals with only a single tick.

This whatsapp techniques are successful relying upon how you use them.

Instagram Sales System: There are three successful approaches to sell on Instagram:

1. Utilizing Insta stories
2. Utilizing Insta bio
3. Utilizing Insta messaging

1. Utilizing Insta stories: This component is limited to individuals with 10k followers, they can share links on their accounts. It's an incredible method for directing people to offers.

2. Insta bio: Anyone can utilize this highlight just by setting an interface on their profile to direct people to their offers.

3. Insta direct messaging: Another method for selling your subsidiary item on Instagram is to advertise the affiliate link through people's DM. By your attentiveness you should know who observes your proposition engaging, don't simply send your link to anybody.

Youtube Selling Technique: I have actually gotten some item utilizing this strategy. I'll be letting you know now. This technique involves giving worth through video content on YouTube. You can utilize your video to clarify what you're marketing and then input your link on the description and direct watchers to exploit your offer.

Sales Funnel: This technique for selling has made me thus many individuals truckload of cash and it is demonstrated to be relied upon given you realize technique well. This is the demonstration of taking expected clients on an excursion to clarify what you are offering. It very well may be in a type of sales page (Text, illustrations or on the other hand video).

Facebook Advertisements: Over 1 billion individuals use Facebook and it's an extraordinary apparatus to drive sales to your offer straightforwardly or to your sales page just by running a paid advertisement with Facebook.

Email Building Technique: With this technique, you can send customized email to individuals however you should initially convince individuals to willingly give you their email. One of the ways of getting individuals email is to give them a gift that they can get to through their email. After which, you can send them customized messages about your offer. Let your lead magnet associate with your offer so you can get the best arrangement of individuals to converse with about your items.

Twitter System: Twitter is different kind of social media platform compared to the rest I've mentioned above. Twitter post doesn't really contain long words and so it's difficult to use a newbie but excellent if you know how to use copywriting technique.

These are sales techniques that have been tried and trusted, you can utilize them to create huge pay with Affiliate Marketing.

SECTION 7

COPYWRITING FOR AFFILIATE MARKETING

Marketing is the core of affiliate marketing and that is the reason one who want progress in affiliate marketing ought to learn copywriting.

Copywriting is composed substance that persuade the crowd to make a move.

Nearly all that you compose inside a business setting could be considered as copy. Words use on Webpages, advertisements, email newsletter, advertising materials, business cards, video scripts, Instagram post, LinkedIn profile, YouTube description and so on.

Wherever you come into contact with a business, copy appears in some structure. Without copy, business can barely impart anything to customers at all.

Copywriting is a consolidation of imagination and science. They are business objective to accomplish our clients to interface with.

COPYWRITING BASICS

In this section, we will cover the nuts and bolts of copywriting especially for online reasons, for example, pages, advertisements, etc. it's simple as the vast majority are on their advanced mobile phone with technology progressions. Comprehend companions, individuals don't read a web-based material similar way they would re-printed material.

It is critical to recollect that web clients are dynamic, not detached. So in the event that they can't track down a justification behind remaining on your page, then, at that point, they will leave. The focusing ability for normal grown-ups is 8 to 10 seconds.

They will be centered on tracking down a specific items, services or on the other hand snippet of data. They might have questions like 'what's in for me'? Will I find what I'm searching for in this page or sites?

Zero in on the specific crowd. Keep in mind, you cannot contact everybody.

Support your copywriting with realities. Let a wolf be a wolf. You must make your copy convincing, albeit not exorbitant. Numerous guest tends to notice when your copy is full of hype and at the moment, they'll back off.

Keep your writing basic. You ought to have the ability to convey key thoughts successfully in a couple of lines of composing.

Now, one may ask: Is it better to have a short or long copy? There's no right or wrong on the length of a copy as long as it is charming, crowd might read to the furthest limit of a long copy. Your audience are comprised of people who have different inclination.

Some might jump at the chance to read and dissect before they made a buy choice, while some like to read the significant point and make a quick choice regardless of whether to purchase or not.

TIPS TO COPYWRITING

To be an excellent copywriter, the following options will help you through;

1. START WITH RESEARCH

Research is the key for thinking of productive thoughts and the right plot for your copywriting. Every marketing specialists in a promoting firm knows the worth of research.

"Research-ignorant copywriters are just as deadly as generals who fail to recognize enemy indications." – GRACE EVE.

What do you research on?

☐ Your target group

☐ Your items

☐ Your competitors

☐ Keyword research

☐ Current trend

The primary essence on your research ought to be on clients. The mark of client research is to comprehend the underlining feeling, conduct, problem areas and want.

Client research assists you with distinguishing the components of your items to your best clients. Without data, you will fail to develop your market on those highlights.

2. ADDRESS YOUR AUDIENCE IN PERSON

In this presence time we live in, the internet is full of scams which actually covers the good people. Individuals don't easily believe whatever you post as long as you don't present yourself as genuine by showing yourself one way or another.

3. MAKE YOUR WRITING VITAL

Do you have the attention of a new client? How would you make your writing stick in the psyche of your client? Do utilize words that associate; tell stories, use relationships, lay out an image, supplant gibberish with basic language.

4. WRITE BASICALLY

Make your message understood and simply and make your clients comprehends your offer of advantages as fast as possible.

5. WRITE YOUR CLIENT PHASE OF MINDFULNESS

The more you know your client and their phase of mindfulness. Your writing digest easily to them.

6. ORGANIZE YOUR COPY WITH A FORMULA

Utilizing a copywriting composing formula will increase your knowledge and privileges actually.

7. MAKING YOUR READERS MISS OUT IF THEY DON'T CHOOSE YOU?

Individuals' don't like the sensation of passing up a great opportunity. Structure your message in such a way they will see the outcome if they don't get the items you are marketing.

8. REPUTATION

Reputation is the trust you get overtime from your audience on your items or services. Reputation can involve assurances, testimonies, years of

THE PSYCHOLOGY OF SELLING

involvement, grants, media rating, media inclusion, etc.

9. TRIGGER FEELINGS

Your crowd are individuals with feelings. Have you heard individuals purchase with feelings?

"People don't act on what they say, think what they say, or feel what they think." – NICK MORGAN

11. PROMISES

Without promises, your writing isn't complete.

"Customers continue to purchase goods whose advertisements assure them of their worth for money, attractiveness, comfort from suffering, social standing, and other things." – GRACE EVE.

SECTION 8

COPYWRITING FORMULA

With copywriting formulas, you can compose your copy quicker and with high probability of progress. Know that unique formula works for various people, content sorts, and composing styles.

SIMPLE GUILDLINES FOR EFFECTIVE COPYWRITING;

1. EDIT YOUR WRITING PROPERLY; when you see a good spelling and grammar, your clients perceive you to be professional and thorough.

2. USE A CONCISE AND CLEAR STRUCTURE; most people scan through your writing before reading them in entirety. To make your copywriting

clear, you need to use paragraph often, make keywords bold and include subheadings.

3. MAKE IT PERSONAL; including a personal touch will make it easier for you to develop relationships with your clients and it helps in building trust and reputation over time.

4. BUT DON'T GET TOO PERSONAL; while trying to be relatable to your clients, you should not get into too much details about your relationship, your property, your work or family.

5. DON'T IMPOSE YOUR BELIEFS AND OPINIONS ON OTHERS; when it comes to moral and political matters, keep in mind that not everyone share your views.

6. SEE YOUR CLIENTS AS PROSPECTIVE CUSTOMERS; respond to each email, message and comment courteously and

quickly. Do your best to offer a satisfactory answer to every question.

Below Are Most Common Copywriting Formulas;

1. Before – After – Bridge

Before – Here's your word...

After – Imagine what it'd be like, having problem solved.

Bridge – Here's how to get there

This is our current go-to formula. Describe a problem, describe a world where that problem doesn't exist, then explain how to get there. Pretty simple setup and can work for copy write-ups, online media posts, email and anywhere.

2. Problem – Agitate – Solve

Identify a **problem**

Agitate the problem

Solve the problem

You're looking at one of the most popular copywriting formulas out there. Writers call this formula the "the key to dominating online medias". It's ever-present in copywriting lists and tips.

3. Features – Advantages – Benefits (FAB)

Features – What you or your product can do

Advantages – Why this is helpful

Benefits – What it means for the person reading

This copywriting formula highlights one of my favorite bits of advice on writing. Focus on benefits, not features.

4. The 4 C's

Clear

Concise

Compelling

Credible

Here's one of my favorite formula because it reminds me to stay focused on the goals of the copy and the benefits to the reader. Keep the writing clear, keep it concise, find a compelling angle to write from, and write with credibility that what you're promising can be trusted to happen.

5. The 4 U's

Useful – Be useful to the reader

Urgent – Provide a sense of urgency

Unique – Convey the idea that the main benefits is somehow unique

Ultra specific – Be ultra-specific with all of the above

Looking for how to write an online media headline? Start here. The 4 U's formula seems ready-made for such. The elements of urgency and specificity fit well with the fast pace of social and the small amount of text. If mastered, you can expect to see great results.

6. Attention – Interest – Desire – Action (AIDA)

Attention – Get the reader's attention

Interest – Interesting and fresh information that appeals to the reader

Desire – Benefits of your product/service/idea and proof that it does what you say

Action – Ask for a response

AIDA is one of the most standard copywriting formulas for most any type of marketing copy. It's been used for direct mail, television and radio, sales pages, landing pages, and so much more.

7. The 5 basic objections

1. I don't have enough **time**.
2. I don't have enough **money**.
3. It won't work for me.
4. I don't believe you.
5. I don't **need** it.

Chances are that a reader can easily come up with reasons not to read or click or share. Those reasons will likely fall one of these five basic buckets. Keep these in mind as you're writing. If you can solve all of them, wonderful. If you can solve even one, great.

These copywriting formulas give a decent aide particularly to get everything rolling with copywriting rapidly. When you write routinely, you get to understand which formula to use a given time. Don't only read this; Take out your note pad and begin rehearsing on utilizing the formulas.

SECTION 9

CONCLUSION

All the business models I've explained in this book is extremely profitable if you put in the work towards achieving the skills required to start the work. Without a positive mindset, it's almost impossible to be successful in any area and that's why the first chapter dealt with mindset extremely.

Affiliate marketing has really changed my life more than I can say to you and it is a good way to earn a living, being your own boss is very interesting, being able to work at your own pace and time. Being able to travel around the world and still work and so other business I've mentioned here.

You need to understand that none of this business will start generating you cash if you don't put in the work, it is not an overnight thing. You need to learn, understand the basics and also adapt to the changes as it comes.

Steady passive income and financial freedom only comes with well-planned and executed activities, goals. Making substantial efforts towards across the social media platforms to display yourself as a credible promoter and business person. Something that every business person wants.